DINOMITE!

All About Dinosaurs

by
Darice Bailer

with
Matthew T. Carrano, Ph.D.
Consultant

Scholastic Inc.

New York Toronto London Auckland Sydney
Mexico City New Delhi Hong Kong Buenos Aires

ISBN 0-439-83862-2

Designers: Lee Kaplan and Julia Sarno.

Cover and title page illustration: *Allosaurus fragilis* © Jaime Chirinos.

Interior graphic illustrations: Ed Shems and Yancey Labat.

All 3-D conversions by Pinsharp 3D Graphics.

Special thanks to Mike Fredericks and Emily Waples for their help on this project.

Interior Photo and Illustration Credits:
Page 4: *Centrosaurus* © H. Kyoht Luterman.
Page 5: Group of *Tyrannosaurus rex* © Julius Csotonyi.
Page 7: *Paralititan* © Todd Marshall.
Page 8: *Apatosaurus* and *Allosaurus* © Melissa Frankford.
Page 10: (Dinosaur skeleton) © Tonis Valing/Shutterstock.com.
Page 11: (Dinosaur egg) © Sam Lee/Shutterstock.com; (reptile skin) © Jeff Gynane/
    Shutterstock.com; (baby alligator) © WizData, Inc./Shutterstock.com.
Page 12–13: (World map) NASA/R; all dinosaur illustrations © John Bindon.
Pages 14–15: All dinosaur illustrations © John Bindon.
Pages 16–17: All dinosaur illustrations © JR Mudyryknow.
Page 18: (*Allosaurus* skull) © B. Speckart/Shutterstock.com; (*Brachiosaurus* skull)
    © Sandy Felsenthal/Corbis.
Page 19: *Allosaurus* © Todd Marshall.
Page 20: Sauropods with *Iguanodon* © Gerhard Boeggemann.
Page 21: (*Brachiosaurus* skeleton) © Jim Jurica/Shutterstock.com.
Page 22: *Tyrannosaurus rex* and *Triceratops* © Joe Tucciarone.
Page 23: (Meteor crater) © Rodney Mehring/Shutterstock.com; (Kluchevskoj volcano)
    © Bychkov Kirill Alexandrovich/Shutterstock.com.
Page 24: *Archaeopteryx* © Todd Marshall.
Page 25: (*Archaeopteryx* fossil) © Bob Ainsworth/Shutterstock.com; (roadrunner) © Paul S. Wolf/
    Shutterstock.com.
Page 27: (Dinosaur exhibit) © Ritu Sainani/Shutterstock.com; (dinosaur fossil) © Steffen Foerster/
    Shutterstock.com.
Page 28: (Geologic map of the Dinosaur Quarry Quadrangle, Uintah County, Utah) produced by
    the U.S. Geological Survey; (excavation of *Protoceratops* skull) © Louie Psihoyos/Corbis.
Page 29: (Dinosaur exhibit) © Dave G. Houser/Corbis; (desert background) © Wilmy van Ulft/
    Shutterstock.com; (desert background) © Hashim Pudiyapura/Shutterstock.com;
    (*Tyrannosaurus rex* skeleton) © Jenny Horne/Shutterstock.com.
Page 30: *Masiakasaurus* © Julius Csotonyi; (Matthew Carrano) by Eric Duneman, courtesy of
    National Geographic Society Funds; (jungle background) © Steffen Foerster/Shutterstock.com.
Page 31: *Herrerasaurus* and *Eoraptor* © Melissa Frankford.
Page 32: *Aucasaurus* © Jorge Blanco.

12 11 10 9 8 7 6 5 4 3 2 1   6 7 8 9 10 11/0

Printed in the U.S.A.

First Scholastic printing, January 2006

TABLE OF CONTENTS

WELCOME TO

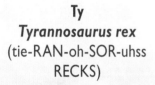

Ty
Tyrannosaurus rex
(tie-RAN-oh-SOR-uhss
RECKS)

Hello and welcome to the world of dinos! My name's Ty, and I'll be tagging along with you as we explore some of the greatest and most spectacular animals that ever walked this planet—that's right, **DINOSAURS!**

As you might know already, dinosaurs were a special group of animals that lived millions and millions of years ago—way before people were around to snap photos!

Join us for a *dino*-mite adventure as we follow the clues to find out more about these prehistoric giants! Did you know that…

◆ Some dinos had heads that were nearly eight feet long?

◆ Some dinos weighed more than 40 tons?

◆ There were dinos with *feathers?*

Centrosaurus
(SEN-troh-SOR-uhss)

3-D Dinosaur Discovery

A group of *Tyrannosaurus rex*

We'll learn **tons** more about dinos as we start out on our first adventure, such as:

- ◆ What are dinosaurs?

  - ◆ What was the world like when dinosaurs lived?

- ◆ How can we find dinosaurs today?

Ready for an adventure? Follow the dinosaur tracks, and let's get started!

DINOS...IN 3-D!

Your **3-D Dinosaur Discovery** book comes with a pair of nifty 3-D glasses to help the dino pictures really come to life. Look at the picture on the next page without your glasses— pretty ordinary, right? Now put on your glasses and look again!

 Keep your 3-D glasses handy when you're reading this book. When you spot this icon, put on your glasses for some eye-popping dino action!

Wow, this picture really **pops!**

Your 3-D Dino Kit

Along with this book and 3-D glasses, you received a slide projector and slides packed with dino pics! Be sure to read the instructions, and with a grown-up's help, set up your projector.

Some of the slides feature dino pics that you'll see in this book. Be a junior paleontologist! Put on a super slide show for your family or friends. They'll be wowed by all the new things you've learned!

You'll also see some other symbols in this book as you go about your dino adventures. Here's a list of what they are and how they'll help you on your way.

 **Dino Dictionary** will point out new words that you might not know. If you find a word that you don't know, look for this symbol!

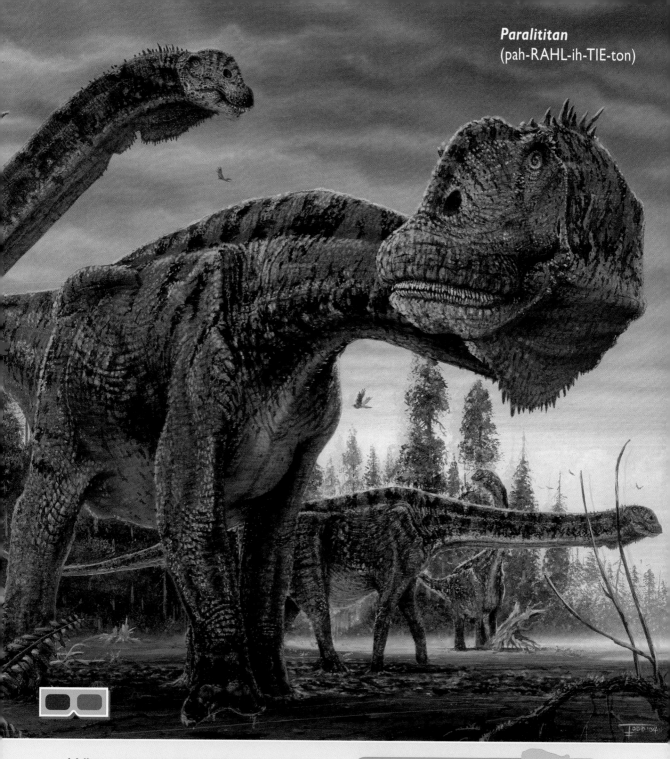

Paralititan
(pah-RAHL-ih-TIE-ton)

When you see **Dino Data**, you'll get a little bit of extra-interesting info!

DINO DATA

Funny Bones

Even fossils could use a laugh! Catch some prehistoric jokes with **Funny Bones**!

DINO 101

It's time to meet some of the most amazing animals that ever lived! We'll go over the basics—everything that a dino expert (like you!) should know.

Dinosaurs were a group of **prehistoric** animals related to reptiles and birds that lived 65 million years ago in the **Mesozoic** (MEZZ-uh-ZOE-ik) **Era**. Back then, reptiles were the biggest animals around—so scientists also call this time "The Age of Reptiles."

Yup, it's true—dinos definitely ruled the planet! There were dinos with sharp teeth and claws, horns, bony plates, spikes, feathers—you name it, and there was probably a dino out there that had it.

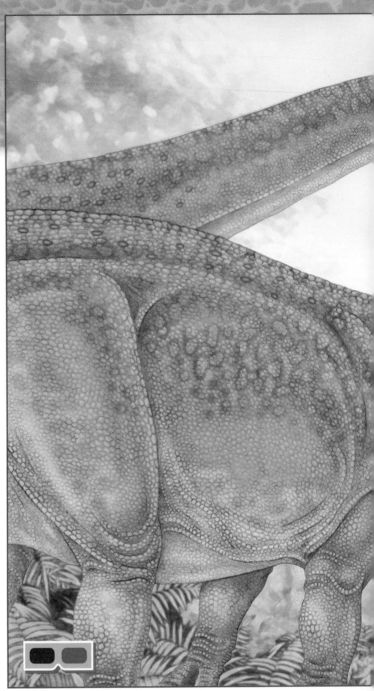

Funny Bones

Q: What do you call a blindfolded dino?

A: A do-you-think-he-*saur*-us!

Dino Dictionary

The word *prehistoric* is used to describe anything that existed before people started writing things down to record history.

Apatosaurus (uh-POT-oh-SOR-uhss) **and *Allosaurus*** (AL-oh-SOR-uhss)

But exactly *how* is a dinosaur different from another reptile, like an alligator? Put on your thinking caps—we're going to be dino detectives and find out!

What Is a Dinosaur?

The name *dinosaur* actually comes from two Greek words—*deinos* means "terrible" and *sauros* means "lizard."

So, were dinosaurs terrible lizards?

Nope! They weren't even lizards! Lizards are *small* reptiles. Dinosaurs are a special group of reptiles with some important differences. Check out these pages to see how a regular reptile and a mighty dino measure up!

Dinosaurs and **reptiles** both have **backbones**.

Dinosaurs had **extra openings in their skulls** to make them lighter and also to make room for powerful jaw muscles.

Saurornitholestes
**(SOR-roar-NITH-oh-LESS-tees)
skeleton**

DINO DATA

A British scientist named Richard Owen made up the word *dinosaur* in 1842. When he said that dinosaurs were "terrible," he didn't mean they were awful. He meant that dinos were so strange that they filled people with terror. Yikes!

Dinos walked on their **toes**. Reptiles (and people!) walk on their heels.

Dinosaur egg

Dinosaurs laid hard-shelled eggs. Some reptiles also lay hard-shelled eggs, but others, like turtles, lay eggs with softer, leathery shells.

Reptile skin

Reptiles have scaly, waterproof skin. Scientists think that **dinosaur skin** was not as scaly, but more like **bumpy leather**.

All reptiles are cold-blooded. But scientists don't really know if dinosaurs were cold-blooded or **warm-blooded**. There could have been both cold- and warm-blooded dinos, and some might have been in between.

Dinosaurs' legs didn't stick out to the sides like reptiles' do. Instead, **the legs came from straight below the dinosaur**. This allowed dinos to run faster, and for some to walk on their hind legs.

Baby alligator

Dino Dictionary

If an animal is *cold-blooded*, it means it needs to use the sun to warm itself, and sits in the shade to cool down. *Warm-blooded* animals can keep themselves warm without using the sun, and use sweat to cool off.

NO SWIMMING (OR FLYING) ALLOWED!

Sorry, but **real dinos were land-based**. They weren't swimmers or fliers. There were some prehistoric animals that flew or swam that looked like dinos, but they really weren't dinos at all. And while some dinos might have taken a dip now and then, none of them had flippers or webbed feet.

It's hard to say when dinosaurs started to appear, but scientists believe it was about 230 million years ago. Dinosaurs hung around for another 160 million years after that first dinosaur walked the Earth!

That's quite a track record!

Triassic

The Triassic Period
(about 252–200 million years ago)

At the beginning of the Triassic, Earth wasn't divided into seven **continents**. Instead, there was one **supercontinent** called **Pangaea** (pan-JEE-uh).

> ### Dino Dictionary
> The word *supercontinent* describes the big piece of land that existed before it was broken up into the seven separate **continents**.

This giant piece of land was very close to the **equator** (e-KWAY-tor)—an imaginary line halfway between the North and South Poles. Also, the weather was dry and hot. Pangaea probably had a lot of deserts.

The first dinosaurs started to appear during the Late Triassic—along with other prehistoric reptiles and small mammals. There were both plant-eating and meat-eating dinos (like *Staurikosaurus*) in the Triassic, but they weren't as big as the dinos in later periods. (Remember, dinos were just starting out!)

Triassic

Staurikosaurus
(staw-REEK-oh-SOR-uhss)

Jurassic

The Jurassic Period
(about 200–146 million years ago)

Over time, Pangaea started to break up. By the end of the Jurassic, Pangaea had split into two pieces called **Gondwana** (gond-WAH-nah) and **Laurasia** (law-RAY-zhah). The weather during the Jurassic was still warm, but not as dry as the Triassic, since more land was near the ocean.

During the Jurassic, more kinds of dinosaurs appeared—including very large plant-eating dinosaurs and armored dinosaurs. These dinos had spines, thick plates, and other stuff for protection. The Jurassic is known for its humongous plant-eaters—like ***Apatosaurus*** and ***Mamenchisaurus*** (mah-MENCH-ih-SOR-uhss), along with some other famous dinos, like ***Stegosaurus*** (STEG-oh-SOR-uhss).

Jurassic

Mamenchisaurus

THE MESOZOIC ERA?

But a lot of things changed during those 160 million years. Even the Earth itself did a bit of rearranging! To help you see what the world was like back in the days of dinos, we'll travel to the three periods of time that make up the Mesozoic: the **Triassic** (try-AH-sick), the **Jurassic** (jure-AH-sick), and the **Cretaceous** (kreh-TAY-shus).

Cretaceous

▲

The Cretaceous Period
(about 146–65 million years ago)

By this time, Pangaea was well on its way to breaking into the continents that we know today with the same seasons. Dinos probably spent their time moving around to find warm weather, just like some animals do today, but others lived near the North and South Poles.

Some large plant-eaters like **Brachiosaurus** (BRACK-ee-oh-SOR-uhss) and **Diplodocus** (dih-PLOD-oh-cuss) died out, but these were replaced with new dinos like **Titanosaurus** (tie-TAN-oh-SOR-uhss). Also, horned dinosaurs—like **Triceratops** (try-SER-uh-tops)— appeared, along with meat-eating dinos big and small, like **Tyrannosaurus rex** and **Velociraptor** (vee-LOSS-ih-RAP-tore).

What's important to know is that not all dinosaurs lived all together at one time. Some dinosaurs were disappearing as new ones appeared. What happened to the dinosaurs after the Cretaceous? Skip to page 22 to see what wiped out these giants of the Mesozoic!

Cretaceous

Tyrannosaurus rex

DINO DATA

A German geologist named Alfred Wegener came up with the supercontinent theory in 1915. He called the supercontinent "Pangaea" because it means "all lands" in Greek.

Where Did Dinosaurs Live?

That's easy...EVERYWHERE!

Yup, that's right! Dinosaur bones have been found on every continent—even Antarctica!

North America

Edmontosaurus
(ed-MON-toe-SOR-uhss)
Late Cretaceous—65 million years ago
Some scientists think this duck-billed dino had loose skin around its nose that it could blow up like a balloon!

Euoplocephalus
(YOO-ah-ploh-SEF-uh-lus)
Late Cretaceous—76 million years ago
This dino was like a tank—it had a bony shield and rows of spikes down its back.

South America

Argentinosaurus
(are-jen-TEEN-oh-SOR-uhss)
Early Cretaceous—99 million years ago
This dino was a huge plant-eater— one of the biggest! Weighing in at 70 tons, it was as heavy as 35 rhinoceroses.

Cryolophosaurus
(KRY-oh-loaf-oh-SOR-uhss)
Early Jurassic—195 million years ago
This meat-eater had a strange triangular crest (or ridge) above its eyes.

ANTARCTICA

If you read pages 12–13 carefully, you might know why. Since Pangaea was one big continent, dinos were able to get all over the world just by walking. No planes or boats for dinos!

Look at the map below to see some of the kinds of dinosaurs that scientists have found all over the world!

Europe

Iguanodon
(igg-WAHN-no-don)
Early Cretaceous—110 million years ago
One of the first dinos to be discovered, scientists goofed when putting this plant-eating dino's bones together. They placed its sharp thumb spike on its nose! Oops!

Asia

Gallimimus (GAL-ih-MY-muss)
Late Cretaceous—75 million years ago
Although its name means "chicken mimic," *Gallimimus* was a lot bigger than a chicken—20 feet (6 m) long!

Africa

Sinosauropteryx
(SINE-oh-sore-OP-tayr-iks)
Early Cretaceous—140 million years ago
One of the first dinos found with fur-like feathers all over its body, probably used to keep it from freezing—not flying.

Elaphrosaurus
(el-LAH-froh-SOR-uhss)
Late Jurassic—155 million years ago
Not much is known about this dino. Scientists think that *Elaphrosaurus* was a fast-running meat-eater.

Australia

Kentrosaurus
(KEN-troh-SOR-uhss)
Late Jurassic—156 million years ago
With its spiky back and hoof-shaped toe claws, the African *Kentrosaurus* looked a whole lot like the North American dino, *Stegosaurus*.

Leaellynasaura
(lee-ELL-in-uh-SOR-uh)
Early Cretaceous—110 million years ago
This dinosaur had large eyes that helped it to see in the long, dark winter evenings.

ANTARCTICA

15

What Kinds of Dinosaurs Are There?

Scientists discovered the first dinosaur nearly 200 years ago, and they're digging up new dino fossils faster than ever. As scientists find new ones, they add them to the dino family tree. Scientists have found around 900 kinds of dinos.

That's a big family reunion!

Scientists divide dinos into two big groups: ones that have hipbones like lizards are called **Saurischian** (saw-RIH-skee-un) dinosaurs. Dinos with hips like birds are called **Ornithischian** (or-nih-THIH-skee-un) dinosaurs.

Look at the chart below to check out the different dino groups.

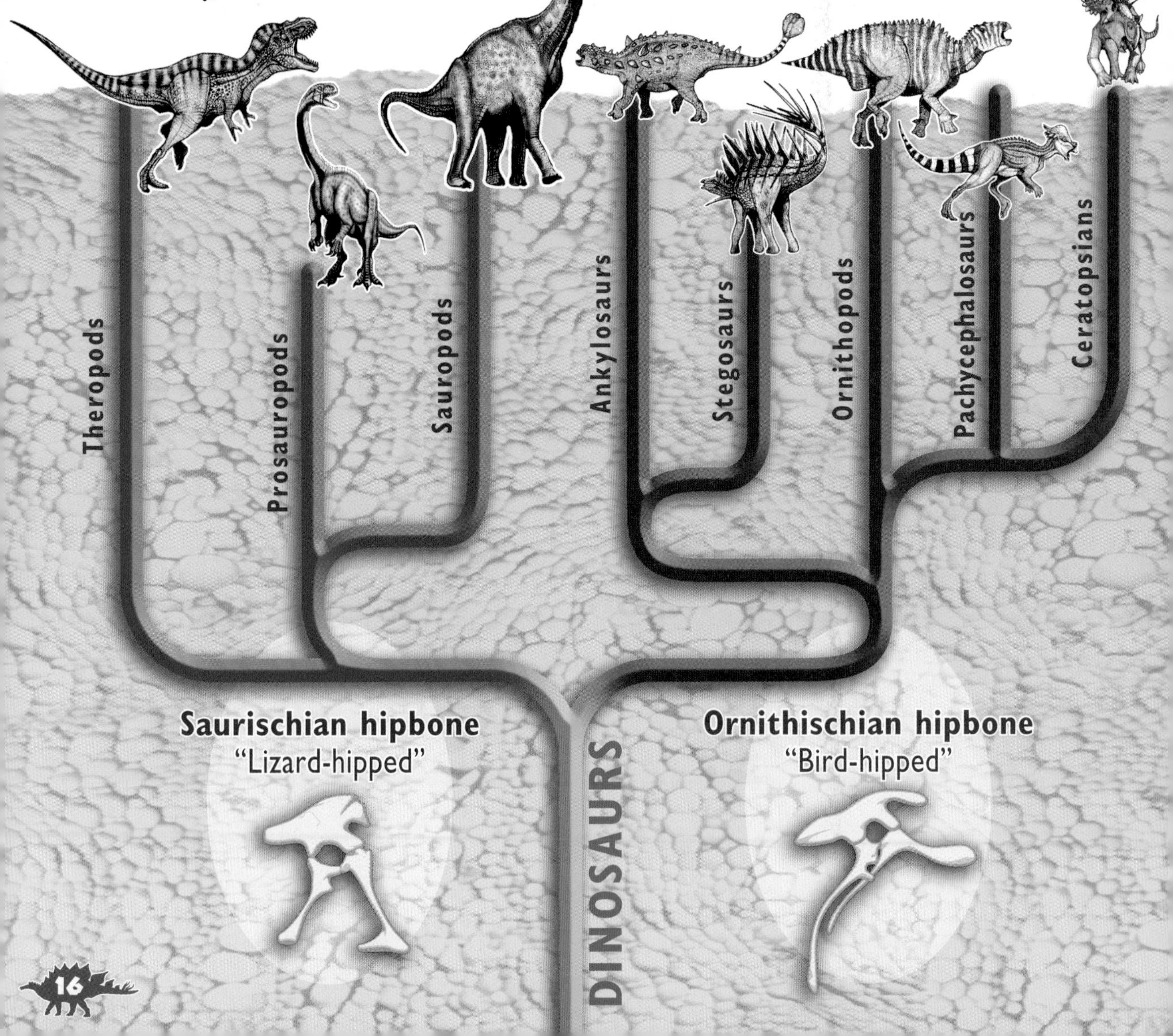

Theropods

Prosauropods

Sauropods

Ankylosaurs

Stegosaurs

Ornithopods

Pachycephalosaurs

Ceratopsians

Saurischian hipbone
"Lizard-hipped"

Ornithischian hipbone
"Bird-hipped"

DINOSAURS

Saurischian Dinosaurs (plant- and meat-eaters)

Theropods (THAYR-oh-pods)
Theropods were meat-eating dinosaurs who walked on two legs, had two arms to grab their prey, and strong jaws and sharp teeth.

Prosauropods (pro-SAW-roh-pods)
Prosauropods were plant-eaters who walked on either two or four legs. They were early cousins of the giant sauropods (see below)—perhaps even their **ancestors**— but were much smaller.

Sauropods (SAW-roh-pods)
Sauropods were some of the biggest animals to walk the Earth—they had very long necks and tails.

Dino Dictionary
An animal's *ancestor* (ANN-sess-tore) is a member of its family that lived a long time ago.

Ornithischian Dinosaurs (plant-eaters)

Ankylosaurs (ang-KYE-loh-SORS)
These dinos had bony shields on their backs. Some had clubs on their tails for defense.

Stegosaurs (STEG-oh-SORS)
Stegosaurs were armored dinosaurs covered from head to tail with bony plates—like a prehistoric mohawk!

Ornithopods (or-NITH-oh-pods)
These dinos were plant-eaters that could walk on either two or four legs. Some were chicken-sized, but others were huge. The largest are called "duck-billed" dinosaurs.

Pachycephalosaurs (PACK-ee-SEFF-a-loh-SORS)
These dinos had thick bones shaped like helmets on their heads. Scientists think that males rammed into each other to compete for females.

Ceratopsians (SER-uh-TOP-see-ens)
This group was made up of the horned dinos. Scientists think that their bony frills protected their necks and were used for showing off to other dinos.

Guess the Dino's Dinner

Look at these two dinosaur skulls. Can you tell which one was a meat-eater and which one was a plant-eater?

Did you figure it out? If you thought that the one on the left belonged to a **carnivore** (KAR-nih-VORE) and the one on the right belonged to an **herbivore** (ER-bih-VORE)—you're absolutely right! Read on to find out more about dino diets.

Meet the Meat-Eaters

The skull of the meat-eater above is from an *Allosaurus*. We'll call him "Al." All meat-eating dinos were from the theropod group—which you learned about on page 17. Here are some juicy tidbits on these prehistoric hunters.

Dino Dictionary

A *carnivore* is any animal that only eats meat. An *herbivore* is any animal that only eats plants.

What Big Teeth You Have!

The jaws of carnivores were very powerful. With sharp, slicing teeth measuring up to four inches (10 cm) long, Al could easily snap up a meal in the Mesozoic. Those jaws and teeth could rip and yank out huge chunks of flesh—and no worries about losing a tooth! If a tooth fell out, another grew in its place.

On the Prowl

Back in the time of dinosaurs, you needed more than a big mouth to be a meat-eater. Just like the meat-eating animals of today, you first needed to be able to *find* or *catch* something to eat.

Al probably knew when a meal was around because he had excellent senses. Perhaps he could sniff them out or hear them coming! Or maybe Al preferred leftovers—weak or sick animals, or ones that were already dead. Once he found his **prey**, Al probably dug into dinner with his long hand and toe claws.

Allosaurus

Mini Meat-Eaters

Not all carnivorous dinos were big and bad. Some dinos like *Velociraptor* were small but speedy hunters. Size isn't everything!

Hooray for Herbivores!

The skull on the right side of page 18 belongs to a *Brachiosaurus*, who lived during the Late Jurassic. Most dinosaurs were herbivores. In fact, there were lots more plant-eating dinos than meat-eaters (look at page 17)! Read on to find out more about some of the biggest dinos that munched their way across the Mesozoic.

Two sauropods with some *Iguanodon*.

Eat Your Veggies

While they didn't have razor-sharp teeth like Al on page 18, herbivores had special chompers, too. Some dinos' upper teeth slid over the lower teeth to grind up leaves and branches. Other dinos had lots of small teeth designed for chewing tough prehistoric plants. Some dinos didn't bother with chewing—they just swallowed their food whole! Those dinos probably swallowed rocks, which ground up the food in their stomachs. Many plant-eaters had cheeks, which helped keep food in their mouths while they chewed it up.

Reach for the Sky

So, if you're a plant-eater, how do you get the best branches and leaves? It helps if you're tall! Lots of herbivores had super-long necks to reach the tasty tidbits on the tops of prehistoric trees. Some scientists think that big herbivores could stand on their back legs to give themselves a boost, too.

Stick Your Neck Out

Long necks were also good for nabbing food lower to the ground. Dinos could stand in one place and just move their heads around to munch. This helped them save a lot of energy while looking for food. Long necks could also get into hard-to-reach places, like in between trees.

Put Your Best Foot Forward

Herbivores usually walked on four legs, since they didn't need arms to grab a meal like carnivores did. Some herbivores were very large and heavy, like *Stegosaurus*. But some plant-eaters, like *Iguanodon*, used their front hands to pick up leafy twigs and stuff them into their mouths.

 Brachiosaurus skeleton

A DINO DISAPPEARING ACT:

Triceratops and
Tyrannosaurus rex

It's safe to say that dinos aren't around anymore—we would've definitely noticed if they were! That's because dinosaurs are **extinct**. So, what happened to these mighty creatures? Well, we don't know.

> ## Dino Dictionary
>
> When an animal is *extinct*, it doesn't exist any more—except in fossil form!

All we do know is that 60 million years ago, something happened that made it impossible for dinos to survive—along with half of all the other creatures living on Earth. What was it? Here are two ideas scientists have come up with.

It Came from Outer Space

Based on samples taken from prehistoric rock, some scientists think that at the end of the Cretaceous, a big rock from outer space called an *asteroid* (AH-steh-royd), slammed into the Earth. Besides putting a really BIG hole in the ground, the asteroid kicked up so much dust that it blocked out the sun!

Hey! Who turned out the lights?

Without the sun, plants shriveled up and died. Without plants, the herbivorous dinos didn't have anything to eat, so they died, too. And without any herbivores to eat, the carnivores couldn't survive, either. In 1991, scientists found a huge crater in Mexico—about 125 miles (200 km) wide. This **crater** might have been from the asteroid that wiped out the dinos.

Turn Up the Heat

Another extinction idea has to do with the breaking up of Pangaea (see page 12) in the Mesozoic. All that land moving around might have caused lots of **volcanoes** to become active—releasing lots of **lava**.

All the volcano eruptions could've caused problems for dinos. Volcanoes don't only spew lava—they send dust and harmful gases into the air, too. All that dust and gas may have caused acid rain, which killed many of the plants that dinos ate. And after the eruptions, the weather might have changed so that the Earth could cool off. Maybe dinos couldn't handle the chilly weather!

Crater

Dino Dictionary

A *crater* (KRAY-ter) is a circle-shaped dent left from an explosion, or when something big and heavy (like an asteroid!) falls on the Earth.

Volcano

Dino Dictionary

A *volcano* is an opening in the earth that releases lava—hot, melted rock.

Birds—Living Dinosaurs?

As you read on pages 22–23, dinosaurs are extinct, but that doesn't mean that they're completely gone! Why is that? Well, that's because scientists think that today's birds are direct descendants of dinos way back in the Mesozoic.

No way! I'm related to—a bird?

Yup, that blue jay you see in your backyard had a dino family way back in the Jurassic. Here's how!

Archaeopteryx

A Feathery Find

Scientists got the idea that dinos and birds might be related from *Archaeopteryx* (AR-kee-OP-teh-ricks), a prehistoric bird that lived 150 million years ago. When *Archaeopteryx* was first discovered in 1861, scientists thought it was just a plain ol' bird. It had wings, feathers, and hollow bones.

In 1865, an English scientist named Thomas Henry Huxley noticed that there were a few things about *Archaeopteryx* that weren't usually found in birds. *Archaeopteryx* had teeth, claws, and a long bony tail—stuff that reptiles (like dinosaurs!) have. Based on *Archaeopteryx*, Huxley came up with the idea that dinos and birds were related.

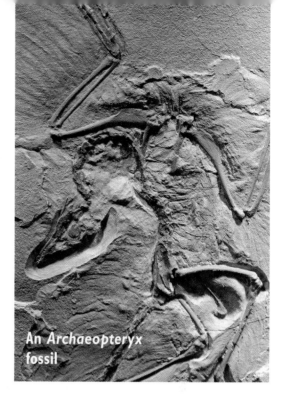
An *Archaeopteryx* fossil

Some scientists think that *Archaeopteryx* looked like this bird called a roadrunner.

Dino Dictionary

Evolution describes how living things slowly change over time in order to survive. Animals evolve in order to live in changing surroundings or *environments*.

Evolution: It's For the Birds

So, how would that happen? Some dinos slowly changed over millions and millions of years to grow feathers and bones light enough to fly. Maybe these changes helped them to be better hunters or live in new places or **environments** (en-VYE-ruhn-muhnts). This process is called **evolution** (eh-vuh-LOO-shun).

While scientists don't think that *Archaeopteryx* was the ancestor of today's birds, *Archaeopteryx* was important because it showed that birds evolved from dinos. Birds you see today are probably descended from smaller meat-eating dinos, like *Velociraptor*. So the next time you see a blue jay, just think—you're looking at a modern-day dino!

If dinos are extinct, how do we know so much about them? Lucky for us, dinos left some clues—**fossils** (FAH-suhls)!

Fossils are leftover parts of plants or animals that lived a long time ago. By finding and studying fossils, scientists can find out what kinds of dinos existed, how they moved, how big they were, and lots more! Read on to find out more about the exciting world of **paleontology** (PAY-lee-uhn-TAW-luh-gee) and how dinos are discovered!

Forming Fossils

Normally, when a living thing dies, its body doesn't hang around for long. If it isn't eaten, it rots away. But for a dino fossil, something special happens. Take a look at the pics below to see how fossils form.

1. A dino dies on a plain next to a lake.

2. The dino's body rots away, leaving the skeleton.

3. The lake floods, dropping sand and mud on the bones.

4. Over time, the dino's skeleton is covered with more layers of dirt and mud.

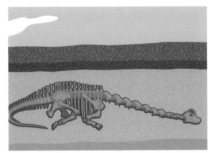

5. Minerals in the ground make the bones super-hard. The dirt and mud around the dino turns to stone.

6. Eventually the fossil is pushed to the surface and is discovered.

DINOS TODAY?

Dinosaur exhibit at a museum

Dino Dictionary

Paleontology is the study of things that lived a long time ago—like dinos! And a **paleontologist** (PAY-lee-uhn-TAW-luh-jist) is a scientist who looks at fossils and tries to see what life was like way back then.

FANTASTIC FOSSILS

Here are the main types of fossils that paleontologists look for:

Body Fossils: Body fossils are made up of hard stuff, like dino bones and teeth. Scientists use them to figure out how old a fossil is and what the dino looked like. Some very rare body fossils are made of soft stuff, like skin or muscles—and sometimes even eggs!

Trace Fossils: Trace fossils are things that weren't bone—stuff like footprints, things found in the dino's stomach, and…poop! Believe it or not, prehistoric poop (or dung) and other trace fossils can tell a lot about a dino! Scientists get clues about what the dino ate and if it lived in groups—stuff that you can't tell from just bones!

Dinosaur fossil

Finding Fossils

Finding fossils is a long and careful process. You don't just start digging in your backyard! Read on to find out more about the science of digging up dinos!

Step 1: Looking for Buried Treasure

Since dinos lived during the Mesozoic Era, that means dino bones are only found in Mesozoic rock. Paleontologists study special maps to find places where this kind of rock is close to the Earth's surface.

A geologic map—the blue and green areas are Mesozoic rock.

Step 2: A Rocky Road

Badlands in Alberta, Canada

Some of the best sites for finding dino fossils are **badlands**—dry, rocky lands with lots of peaks and ridges. Here, wind or water will wear away the stone or dirt on top of a fossil. Paleontologists visit the site and keep their eyes peeled for anything that looks like a bone—more of the dino's skeleton might be nearby!

Step 3: Draw the Dino

Once paleontologists find a fossil, they work carefully to make sure that it isn't damaged or lost. First, they draw or take pictures of the fossil site to keep track of every piece of bone that they find. They also write down where they found the fossil, how big the bones are, and other info that will help piece together the dino back in the lab.

Step 4: Dig Up the Dino

Once everything is recorded, paleontologists use jackhammers, drills, picks, and brushes to get rid of the rock around the fossil. But paleontologists

A paleontologist uncovers a *Protoceratops* (pro-toe-SER-uh-tops) skull

leave the bones halfway in the rock to protect them when they're traveling to the lab. They also paint special chemicals onto the bones and cover them with newspaper and plaster to be extra safe.

Step 5: In the Lab

The work isn't over once the fossils are at the lab! Paleontologists use smaller tools, like dentists' drills, to chip away the rest of the rock around the fossil. Sometimes they use chemicals that dissolve the rock right off. Work at the lab takes a long time—sometimes longer than it took to dig up the fossil!

A paleontologist works on a _Stegosaurus_ skeleton

Step 6: Putting the Puzzle Together

In order to not damage the bones, scientists make a mold or copy of the fossils and put them together. Since it's rare to find a complete skeleton, scientists do some guessing and make fake bones to put in. Then, the skeleton might be put on display in a museum, or kept for further study.

NAME THAT DINO!

Do you wonder how dinos get their names? Some scientists name dinos after the places they were found—like _Utahraptor_, which was found in Utah. Other scientists might name dinos after themselves or their kids (like _Leaellynasaura_ on page 15)! But most names use Greek or Latin words to describe the dino. Look at the chart to see some examples.

Word	Meaning
Cerato-	horn
Bronto-	thunder
Mega-	great
Micro-	small
Ornitho-	bird
Raptor-	robber
Rex-	king

Tyrannosaurus rex skeleton

If they named a dino after you, what would it be called?

PALEONTOLOGIST
MATTHEW T. CARRANO

Meet Matthew T. Carrano, a paleontologist with the Smithsonian Institution in Washington, D.C. Dr. Carrano has been studying dinosaurs for the last 15 years and has traveled all over the world looking for fossils and making new discoveries. Read on to get the scoop on what it's like to be a paleontologist.

Q **What does a paleontologist do?**

A A paleontologist studies ancient life of all kinds—plants, animals, even bacteria—and how this life appeared, evolved, and went extinct.

Q **Why is it important to learn about dinosaurs?**

A It's important to learn about dinosaurs because they're a great example of many important aspects of evolution. They started out small, evolved to rule the Earth, and then nearly all of them went extinct. One remarkable group—birds—learned to fly, while others reached enormous sizes.

Q **What surprises you the most about dinosaurs?**

A Dinosaurs are always surprising, because we're always learning new things about them. Every year brings us new species from new places, and shows us new shapes and sizes of dinosaurs. The most surprising thing to me is that there are so many kinds of dinosaurs, from a huge sauropod to a tiny hummingbird.

Q **What's your favorite place to dig for fossils?**

A I love visiting other countries and looking for fossils, because it's usually a very interesting and new experience for me. But in the United States, my favorite places to dig are Montana and Wyoming.

Q **What's the weirdest dinosaur you've ever found?**

A *Masiakasaurus* (muh-SHEE-ka-SOR-uhss), a bizarre theropod from Madagascar. *Masiakasaurus* was small—about 5 feet (1½ m) long—and walked on two legs. Its front teeth pointed straight forward out of its mouth, unlike any other dinosaur's.

Masiakasaurus

EORAPTOR

Back in 1991, a paleontologist was on a dig in Argentina. He was about to throw away a piece of rock, thinking it was nothing special, when he noticed some teeth sticking out. When the scientist looked closer, he discovered a little skull. It was so small that it fit in the palm of his hand! The scientist had come face to face with one of the earliest known dinos to strut around on its toes. That fossil was roughly 230 million years old!

230 million years? That's a lot of candles for a birthday cake!

The scientist named it **Eoraptor** (EE-oh-RAP-tore), which means "dawn thief," since it was one of the oldest known dinos at the time that it was discovered. *Eoraptor* wasn't very big at all—only a little over three feet (1 m) tall. It was a carnivore which probably hunted and ate small lizards and ran on its hind legs. It was tough, fast, and successful—one of the reasons that these new dinos evolved and ruled the land. *Eoraptor* definitely had features that later dinosaurs shared, like a light skull, saw-like teeth, and hollow bones. There are so few complete skeletons from this ancient time that *Eoraptor* helped scientists learn many things about how dinos lived at the beginning of the Mesozoic.

Herrerasaurus ▶
(huh-RARE-uh-SOR-uhss)

Eoraptor
▼

MORE DINO ADVENTURES COMING SOON!

Well, we've come to the end of our first adventure. It's been quite the trip! We've covered all the dinosaur basics, seen some fantastic dinos up close, and found out a bit about how scientists study dinos today. But our journey into the world of dinosaurs isn't over yet! We'll head back to the Mesozoic for more exploring. Soon we'll meet the fastest and biggest dinos, learn about dino defenses, take a peek at some dinosaur babies, and we'll dust off some bones on a dinosaur dig.

See you soon—and until then, hope all your adventures are **DINO-mite!**

Aucasaurus
(OW-kah-SOR-uhss)